ELVIS
The King Lives

John Alvarez Taylor

GALLERY BOOKS
An imprint of W.H. Smith Publishers Inc.
112 Madison Avenue
New York, New York 10016

Published by Gallery Books
A Division of W H Smith Publishers Inc
112 Madison Avenue
New York, NY 10016

Produced by
Brompton Books Corp
15 Sherwood Place
Greenwich, CT 06830

ISBN 0-8317-2750-0

Printed in Hong Kong

10 9 8 7 6 5 4 3 2

PHOTO CREDITS
All photos are courtesy the author except:
© RE DeJauregui 112
Las Vegas News Bureau 67, 96
© Lorimar Telepictures 107
Mississippi Department of Economic Development 6
Nixon Presidential Materials Project 98
Nudie's Rodeo Tailors 28
RCA 7, 33, 45, 51, 53, 102
US Department of Defense 32, 40 (top)
Wide World Photos 106
© Bill Yenne 109

Page 1: Elvis Presley, the 'King of Rock and Roll.' In his foreshortened career, he sold over 600 million singles and albums, and starred in 33 motion pictures which in and of themselves grossed $150 million at the box office. *Pages 2—3:* Elvis, in a still from the 1964 Metro-Goldwyn-Mayer motion picture **Viva Las Vegas**. *Page 5:* A 1956 publicity still from Elvis' first motion picture, the block-buster Twentieth Century Fox production of **Love Me Tender**.

INTRODUCTION

Elvis Aron Presley was born at 12:20 pm on 8 January 1935, the son of Vernon and Gladys Presley, in East Tupelo, Mississippi. Elvis was not alone at first—he had a twin, Jesse Garon, but little Jesse died that very day.

The house in which Elvis grew up was built by Vernon, with the help of a $180 loan for materials to build it. Vernon, Gladys and little Elvis often went to the Assembly of God Church on Adams Street in Tupelo, not far from their house, where the Presleys joined the congregation in the singing of hymns—an aspect of the services that Elvis grew to love as he got older.

It was the time of the Great Depression, and the Presleys were exceedingly poor. Elvis remembered hearing his father sobbing because he hadn't enough money to meet the bills. Vernon tried cotton farming at first, then fell into an endless succession of short-term jobs. Gladys worked in a dress factory and took in laundry on the side.

This situation had a strong effect on Elvis—he was especially close to his mother, and seeing her health failing as a result of the family's difficult circumstances strengthened Elvis' resolve to help his parents financially, as soon as he was old enough to to do so. Little could he have dreamed then of the means by which he would one day *truly* help the family financial situation!

In October 1946, Elvis' fifth grade teacher at Lawhan Grade School, Mrs Grames, entered him in a talent contest at the Mississippi-Alabama Fair and Dairy Show. Elvis sang the ballad 'Old Shep,' and won the second place prize of five dollars. This was his first public performance, and was broadcast over WELO radio. Legend has it that Vernon heard this radio broadcast as he was driving a truck on yet another arduous temporary job.

Vernon bought Elvis his first guitar—a $12.95 model purchased from a hardware store—upon Elvis' eleventh birthday, 8 January 1946. The Presleys had, by now, lost their house and the bills just kept piling up. They stayed on, trying to eke out a living in Tupelo until September 1948, when Vernon was inspired to take them to Memphis, where the labor market was beginning a resurgence. There, they moved into a two-bedroom house at 572 Poplar Avenue.

Being just 13 and deep in the shyness of adolescence, Elvis had difficulty making friends in this new locale. He spent a lot of time by himself, singing and playing his guitar. At age 16, he began styling his hair in the 'ducktail' fashion then mostly worn by kids who were considered 'wild.' His sideburns added to this striking effect, and while he did not make the football or baseball team at OC Hume High School—which he now attended—he did enroll in the ROTC program, staying with that for a few years.

His real love was music—especially the songs he heard on the local stations, which featured blues, gospel and country music. After school, he swept floors at Marx Metal Products and was an usher at Lowes State Theater. At home, he practiced his singing, and near the end of his senior year (March 1953), appeared in the OC Hume High School annual variety show.

For his four-song performance, Elvis alternated slow ballads and up-tempo rhythm pieces, ending with a particularly fast number that caused near-pandemonium in the audience. It was but a harbinger of concerts to come.

The family financial situation was still tight, and Elvis began driving a truck for Crown Electric Company after graduation. Then Vernon hurt his back during one of his grueling jobs, and could no longer effectively be a manual laborer. Meanwhile, Gladys had gone to work in a hospital, scrubbing floors and making beds. Her health had worsened, and she was severely taxed by this work.

Elvis' $35 per week as a truck driver would barely cover the family's needs, and he desperately sought a way to help his parents. One day, while driving the Crown Electric truck, he came upon Sun Records Company, which (as a talent-scouting gimmick) offered to record anyone's songs for a four-dollar fee.

Elvis thought that a record of his voice would help to cheer his mother—as her birthday was approaching. Elvis recorded 'My Happiness' and 'That's When Your Heartache Begins.' He returned to record at Sun Records a year later, and so impressed Sun's owner, Sam Phillips, that he signed Elvis to a recording contract.

Elvis' first hit was 'That's All Right, Mama': the legend began.

Above: Elvis was born in this small frame house—built by his father, Vernon Presley, in Tupelo, Mississippi. On 8 January 1935, Gladys Presley gave birth to twins, Elvis Aron (the original spelling) and Jesse Garon. Jesse survived just a few hours.

Facing page: Elvis the star, shortly after he left Sun Records for RCA.

Above: Elvis and his mother, Gladys, in the kitchen of the Presley home in Memphis. It was during the late Depression era that they lost their home in Tupelo, staying on in that municipality for some years afterward. In 1948, Vernon Presley discerned that more money was to be made in the city of Memphis and they moved. Elvis loved his mother, and chanced his first recording to see if he could cheer her up for her birthday.

On 16 October 1954, Elvis became a regular on the **Louisiana Hayride**, an entertainment show similar to the **Grand Old Opry**. Elvis had made his only appearance on the latter show a month earlier, on 25 September, and was not asked to return. Based in Shreveport, Louisiana, the **Hayride** offered Elvis steady work at a salary big enough that he could at last quit his job as a truck driver at Memphis' Crown Electric Company, and become a full-time professional musician.

Facing page: Elvis in a live appearance on the **Louisiana Hayride**, sometime in late 1954 or early 1955.

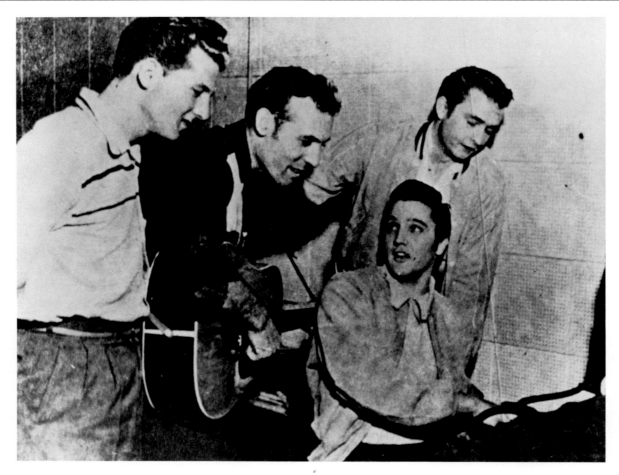

Sam Phillips signed Elvis Presley to a three-year contract with Sun Records on 19 July 1954. Sun was, at the time, the recording label for Jerry Lee Lewis, Carl Perkins and Johnny Cash — all destined for stellar careers.

Above: In the Sun studios, circa 1954–55: Elvis is at the piano, surrounded by (left to right) Jerry Lee Lewis, Carl Perkins and Johnny Cash. At Sun, Elvis recorded a number of legendary cuts, including 'Mystery Train.' He did not stay with Sun Records very long. After a six-month tour of Texas, Arkansas and Louisiana as 'The Hillbilly Cat,' and his appearances on **Louisiana Hayride**, he had become much more than a local Memphis sensation, and RCA Victor bought his contract from Sun in November 1955.

In January of 1956, at RCA's Nashville studios, Elvis laid down the tracks for 'I Got a Woman,' 'Money, Honey' and 'Heartbreak Hotel.' At the end of that month, he flew to RCA's New York studios to lay down tracks for 'Lawdy Miss Clawdy,' 'Shake, Rattle and Roll,' 'Tutti Frutti' and 'Blue Suede Shoes.'

Facing page: A meditative Elvis considers what the future might hold. Despite his already phenomenal popularity, no one, even then, would have predicted that Elvis Presley would become the most popular entertainer in the world, and would influence pop music to such an extent that The Hillbilly Cat would become known as 'The King of Rock and Roll.'

Between 28 January and 24 March 1956, Elvis appeared six times on the Dorsey Brothers **Stage Show**. *Above*: A still from the **Stage Show** — Elvis with Tommy and Jimmy Dorsey, leaders of the legendary Dorsey Brothers Band. The Dorsey Brothers were already headliners in the pop music field when Elvis was still in diapers, and as 'kings of swing,' they were the logical predecessors to Elvis and other rock and rollers.

The **Stage Show** was a nationally-televised entertainment medium, and Elvis' appearances on it would make him a national star. It is indicative of his then-growing reputation that his payment for appearing *six* times on the **Stage Show** was $7500, while just one week after these appearances, he was paid $5000 for a *single* appearance on the **Milton Berle Show**.

In that same week, Elvis was reviewed in the *New York Times*, and was signed to a $450,000 contract with Paramount Pictures to do three movies under the direction of Hal Wallis.

Above: Elvis, as 'Tumbleweed' Presley, during a Wild West skit on the **Steve Allen Show** in 1956. Behind him are Andy Griffith, Imogene Coca and Steve Allen himself. Elvis' stage antics had received bad press, and he had to restrain his performances during the show.

Elvis was once told by a doctor that he used as much energy in a 30-minute performance as a manual laborer does in an eight-hour day! One of Elvis' recurrent nightmares during his meteoric climb to the top of the entertainment industry was, 'Is it all going to last?' Despite the apparent abandon he displayed on stage, Elvis was known to be an exceedingly polite man in person, never failing to say 'Yes, sir' or 'Yes, ma'am.'

Above: Elvis found himself the center of intense attention, and found himself wealthier than his wildest dreams. He signed 'Colonel' Tom Parker as his agent in mid-March 1956, and by the year's end, he and Colonel Parker had made three million dollars. Parker restlessly promoted Elvis, getting him spots on such television variety shows as Ed Sullivan's **Toast of the Town** show.

His recording career was likewise skyrocketing. During the remainder of 1956, Elvis recorded three dozen tracks, including 'Love Me Tender,' 'Don't Be Cruel,' 'Ready Teddy,' 'Rip It Up,' 'Long Tall Sally' and his greatest hit ever: 'You Ain't Nothin' But a Hound Dog.'

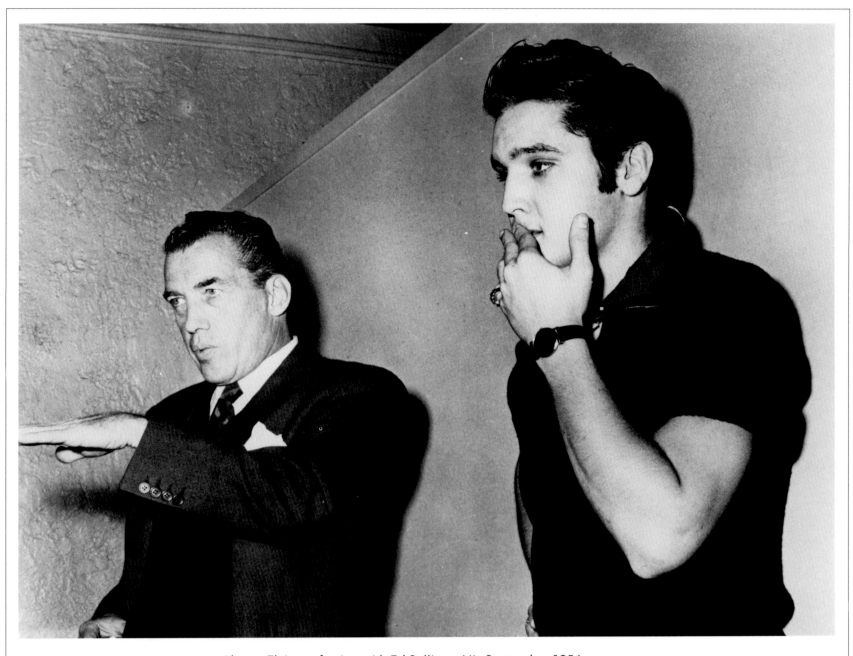

Above: Elvis conferring with Ed Sullivan. His September 1956 appearance on the Ed Sullivan **Toast of the Town** show was controversial: due to increasing social pressure to tone Elvis' act down, Ed Sullivan instructed his cameramen to use tight shots of the singer's upper torso and guitar.

Elvis resented it, saying that if he had to depend on his singing and guitar playing alone, 'I'd be back driving a truck in Memphis at $35 a week.' It turns out that he was wrong; very shortly, he would never have to drive a truck again.

In fact, Elvis was soon to embark on his movie career with the making of the powerfully emotional **Love Me Tender**, which began production on 22 August 1956.

Above: 'The King' prepares to meet his growing numbers of fans. In 1956, he was often doing three to five shows per day, and could not unwind until well after one o'clock in the morning.

Said Elvis, 'Back in Tupelo and Memphis, when Dad and me would go to the carnivals, I used to dream of having enough money to try every game and ride on every ride. Now I got the money, but a big crowd collects around me, and I've got to leave.'

Facing page: Another shot of Elvis as a young rock-and-roll hero. Colonel Parker was doing an unparalleled marketing blitz on the new star, and by year's end, there were Elvis Presley pens, pencils, dolls, greeting cards, bubble gum cards, pins, buttons, pillows, combs, hairbrushes, bookends, guitars, colognes, shoes, wallets and every article of clothing that one could imagine, not to mention lipstick in your favorite shades: Hound Dog Orange, Heartbreak Hotel Pink and Tutti Frutti Red.

Above: A rakish-looking Elvis, posed upon a ladder for the benefit of his many fans. Not everybody liked him — in fact, a lot of country boys like himself resented his popularity with the girls they knew. At one concert, police rounded up a gang of 50 youths who were poised to beat him up after the show.

Even so, such negative reactions did not stop Elvis. His main purpose was to see to it that his mother and father never wanted for money again in their lives.

Facing page, above: Elvis with The Jordanaires. In the studio, Elvis worked slowly and meticulously, exercising a perfectionism that has few parallels in pop music. On stage, he carried his carefully crafted songs to the audience with an uncanny ability to reduce his fans to babbling hysteria with a shiver, a twitch and a burning look; and *then* he unleashed a frenzied intensity that hadn't been seen since the medicine/minstrel shows that drove audiences to fits in the rural, turn-of-the-century South.

Facing page: Elvis, burning up the concert stage, with lead guitarist Scotty Moore and bassist Bill Black in the background.

It certainly wasn't all adulation for the young star. Once, when standing in front of a record store with disk jockey Don Neale, a group of former friends passed by, with barely a response to Elvis' greeting. There were tears in his eyes as he said, 'Now what's eatin' them? I went to school with those kids. They were my friends and now they won't even stop to pass the time of day.'

Above: Elvis Presley, perfectionist, trying out a technique on the drums.

Facing page: A smoldering keg of dynamite. This pose had such appeal that nearly every rock star since has had at least one portrait of themselves done in imitation.

The coat is one he wore ⌐ften in 1957, when the name Elvis Presley was being echoed from every corner of the globe. Colonel Parker's 'Elvis' tee shirts were to be found from the mountain villages of Tibet to the jungles of New Guinea, and Japan was absolutely in an Elvis Presley frenzy.

Above: Elvis strolling, with a menacing coolness, across the driveway of Graceland, the sprawling southern mansion Elvis had bought for he and his parents to live in. Located on US Highway 51 on the south side of Memphis, Graceland and its extensive grounds cost Elvis $100,000 in March 1957. The neighbors felt that the Presleys were model neighbors, but the hundreds of fans that crowded the estate's perimeter walls at any hour of the day or night were another matter altogether.

Facing page: Elvis dressed in black, at one of the countless concerts he played in 1956—57. Alternately frenzied and subdued, his stage persona held audiences ever on the edge of expectancy—who could tell what he would do next?

In 1957, Elvis had the following songs in the Top Ten: 'Jailhouse Rock,' 'All Shook Up,' 'Let Me Be Your Teddy Bear' and 'Too Much.'

Elvis, the phenomenally popular young rock and roller, was always besieged by promoters and agents — all of them trying to 'get a piece of the action.'

Above: Elvis, Colonel Parker (with hat) and a bevy of businessmen and production personnel.

Facing page: Elvis and two more professional types. The one on the left seems to be handing him a business card.

His first release with Sun Records — 'That's All Right, Mama' — back in July of 1954 — sold 20,000 records. By the end of 1956, after he had gone over to RCA from Sun, Elvis was a world-class phenomenon. His records accounted for more than half of RCA's total sales — more than seven million dollars gross.

It was only the beginning.

Above: The usual scene at the stage door after an Elvis Presley concert in the late 1950s. Though he seemed alternately seductive and menacing on stage, Elvis was always polite when signing autographs for his millions of fans. He said of his public that they were 'as nice as could be.'

Facing page: Elvis' appeal was extraordinarily broad, yet it all came down to such moments as this, when a youthful admirer approached him and asked him to sign the dust jacket of his latest hit.

Below: More autographs. In some ways, Elvis loved being able to give people what they wanted. Colonel Parker had millions of extremely varied photographs made of Elvis, to match his moods, and to appeal to every kind of fan. Elvis was presented, variously, as clean-living 'boy next door' and as a lothario; as a good guy and as a villain—the photographs were everywhere one looked.

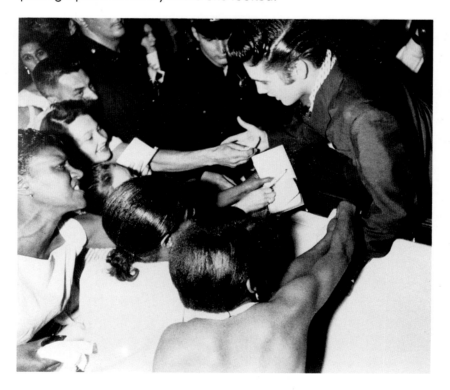

Above: Elvis, with Mr Nudie, of Nudie's Rodeo Tailors—outfitters for major music stars. Nudie has just tailored the gold suit that Elvis is wearing: it was a special award to him from RCA, for being their top recording star. Elvis would wear this suit on the cover of his 1960 album *Fifty Million Fans Can't Be Wrong*.

Above: Elvis from his early days with RCA. This promotional photo shows Elvis in a soft light that is, even so, much less soft than his later image. You can still sense a rawness here, over and above the fact that Elvis' facial features seem to have been designed for dramatic purposes.

Drama was Elvis' next venture into the spotlight of the world. The contract he had signed with Hal Wallis included motion picture companies such as Twentieth Century Fox, Metro-Goldwyn-Mayer and Paramount Pictures. The first film to be produced under this contract was the Twentieth Century Fox blockbuster **Love Me Tender**, a Civil War period piece released in November 1956.

Elvis, as Clint Reno, stays on the family farm while brother Vance Reno (Richard Egan) goes off to fight in the war. Word comes that Vance has been killed in action, and Clint falls in love with Vance's suddenly-bereft fiancee Cathy (Debra Paget). The two marry, only to discover that Vance had not really been killed, and Vance returns. The animosity between the two brothers results in Clint's death — a tear-jerking ending that had women from 18 to 80 sobbing in theaters around the world.

Above: Elvis as Clint and Debra Paget as Cathy in a scene still from **Love Me Tender**, titled for the hit song Elvis performed in the movie.

Facing page: Elvis and producer Hal Wallis at the Twentieth Century Fox studio refectory — Elvis looks as if they have just told him they don't serve deep-fried peanut butter sandwiches (a favorite food).

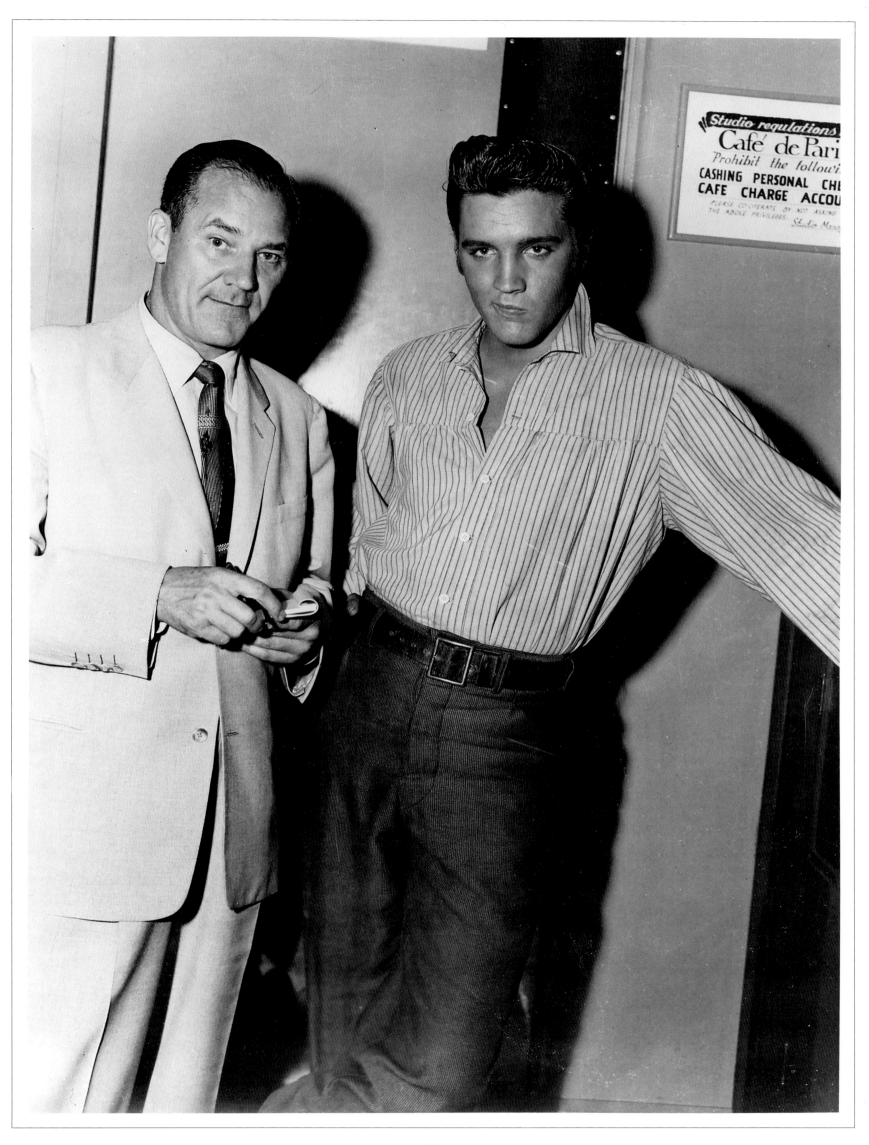

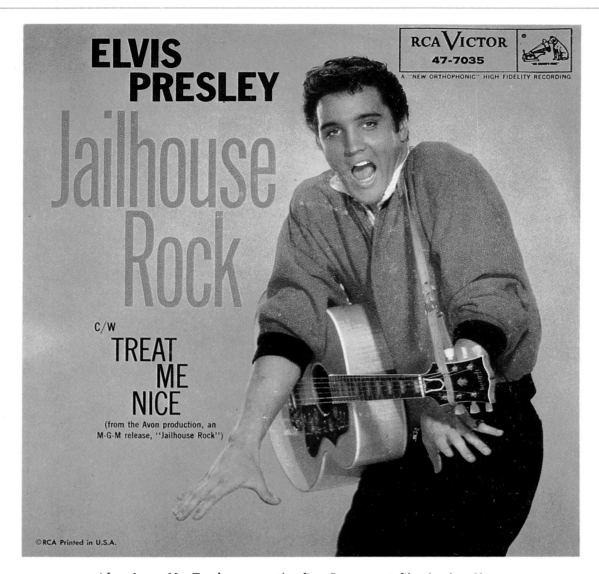

After **Love Me Tender** came the fine Paramount film **Loving You**—
released in July 1957—which mirrored Elvis' own rise to fame, and co-
starred Lizabeth Scott, Wendell Corey and Dolores Hart. The film also
featured an audience shot that revealed Elvis' mom and dad, Gladys
and Vernon, among the 'extras.'

Then came one of Elvis' best-known movies, **Jailhouse Rock**, a
Metro-Goldwyn-Mayer rave-up that was released in October 1957.
Elvis played Vince Everett, a mean, egotistical kid who draws a sen-
tence for manslaughter after accidentally slaying a bully in a bar
brawl. While he's in jail, Hunk Houghton, his cellmate (Mickey Shau-
ghnessy) teaches him to sing and play the guitar. Somehow (and in echo
of the legendary 'Leadbelly's' fame while behind bars), Vince has a
huge following before he even leaves the jail. He goes out, becomes a
huge, cynical success and has to be beaten up by the now-freed Hunk
Houghton before he comes to his senses and marries his ill-treated
sweetheart, Peggy Van Alden (played by Judy Tyler).

Above: A record jacket for the hit single, backed with another tune from
Jailhouse Rock: 'Treat Me Nice.'

Facing page: Elvis as jailbird Vince Everett, in a production number
from **Jailhouse Rock**.

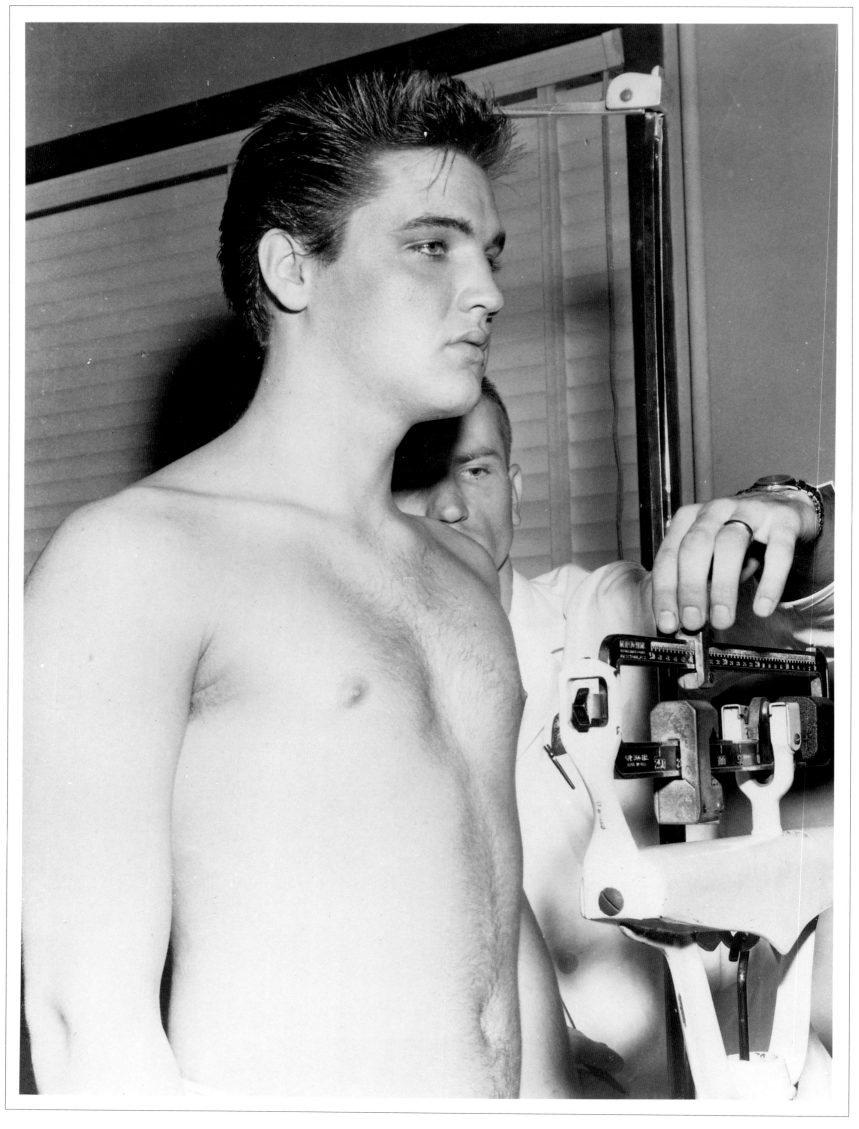

Elvis Presley becomes a soldier. Elvis' next film was perhaps his best: **King Creole**. In his role as Danny Fisher, Elvis proved that he could match the substantial acting talents of co-stars Carolyn Jones, Dolores Hart, Vic Morrow, Dean Jagger and Walter Matthau. However, the US Selective Service interfered, and Elvis had to get a two-month deferment in order to finish the film—completed in March 1958 and released by Paramount in May 1958. On 24 March 1958, Elvis reported to the Memphis induction center. On 25 March, he arrived in Fort Chaffee, Arkansas for a physical *(facing page)* and a haircut. Though a regular GI, he still signed autographs *(below)*. It was not, however, 'goodbye' *(above)* for Elvis Presley.

It was widely speculated that Elvis would probably be put in a Special Services unit, as were most other entertainers that had been inducted, and would spend his tour of duty entertaining the troops. However, Elvis specifically requested to be put in an armored unit, and thus he served his country in much the same way as did millions of other young men.

While he was in boot camp, he received an urgent message from Memphis: Gladys was sick. He received a special leave to visit her, and on 14 August 1958 — two days after his arrival — she died of a heart attack at age 46.

He shortly afterward completed basic training at Fort Hood, Texas, and on 19 September 1958, was assigned to Combat Command C of the Third Armored Division — the 'Mailed Fist' of NATO, and was stationed in the town of Friedburg, West Germany, where he was to be stationed for the remainder of his tour of duty.

Above: Eventually, he became Sergeant Elvis Presley. He is shown here during 'Winter Shield' exercises near the East German border. With him are Private Lonnie Wolfe, manning the wheel, and Specialist Fourth Class Hal Miller, manning the machine gun.

Facing page, above: Elvis at the USO club.

Facing page: Private Elvis Presley still found time to do some entertaining in his off-duty hours. Elvis was considered an 'OK Joe' — in other words, he performed his duties as a soldier and had good camraderie with his fellow GIs.

Above: Elvis in transit—but is he coming closer or going away?

Facing page: Here, he tentatively plucks a string of his guitar: how long would it be until he played before an audience again? In August 1959, Elvis visited the Eagles Club, a social club for American service families. There, he met Priscilla Beaulieu, the step-daughter of US Air Force Captain Paul Beaulieu.

Because Elvis was 10 years older than Priscilla, her stepfather objected at first—but, convinced that Elvis was apparently not like his stage self in private life, he let the two continue their relationship. Elvis was to depart West Germany for home in the spring of 1960. Until then, he had his new-found love—and the US Army—to deal with.

Elvis comes home. Priscilla tearfully accompanied him to Wiesbaden Airport on 2 March 1960, where Colonel Parker took over.

Above: A homecoming press conference.

Facing page: Elvis waves goodbye to West Germany. On 3 March, he stepped off the plane at McGuire Air Force Base in New Jersey *(below)*. In the background—Colonel Parker.

Elvis' popularity hadn't suffered at all through his absence for military duty, thanks to RCA's releasing of tunes he had recorded previous to his US Army service. These included 'You Ain't Nothin' But a Hound Dog,' 'All Shook Up' and 'It's Now or Never.'

It was time to go back to movie making, which 'civilized' his image to even more broadly acceptable levels. Some of these films were quite good, while others degenerated into the sheerest pap.

His first film upon re-entry to civilian life was **GI Blues**, which spawned the hit single 'Wooden Heart.' In this film, Elvis plays a young GI stationed in West Germany. An enterprising young tank driver, he gets his own combo going in his leave time, and falls in love with a West German dancer named Lili (Juliet Prowse). Elvis' character's name is given by *Variety* as Tulsa MacAuley, despite the fact that his name tag in the movie still *on the facing page* gives him a different identity. Undoubtedly, that smile is Elvis' 'glad to be back home' happiness breaking through the characterization.

Above: Elvis and Juliet Prowse, in a publicity still as Tulsa and Lili. Paramount Pictures released **GI Blues** in October 1960.

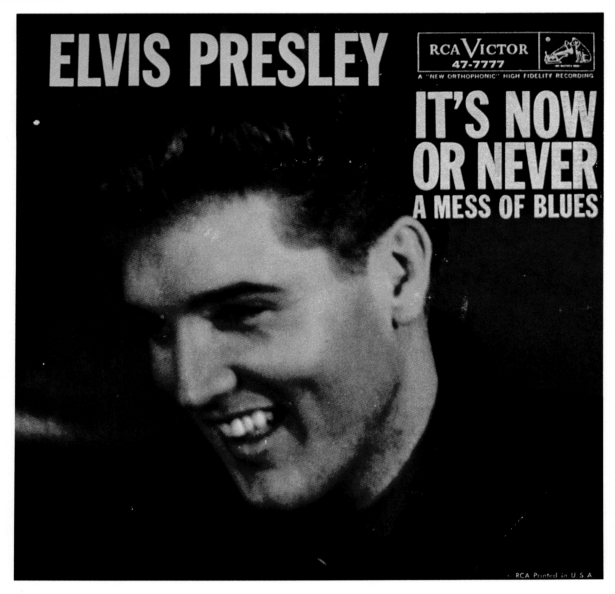

His first hits after the Army were 'Stuck on You' and 'Such a Night,' followed closely by 'It's Now or Never.' Then came the crooning ballad with the spoken bridge that practically shook the charts off the walls: 'Are You Lonesome Tonight?'

Even so, with a heavy movie schedule taking up his time for the foreseeable future, Elvis might well have been wondering if he would ever take to the stage again.

Above: The cover of the hit single 'It's Now or Never,' backed with 'A Mess of Blues.'

Facing page: An introspective Elvis.

Facing page and above: Elvis in his element. Another of his accomplishments in his already crowded life of 1960—61 was the release of an LP of religious songs entitled *His Hand in Mine.* Along with this came several more singles: 'Surrender,' 'Wild in the Country,' 'I Feel So Bad,' 'Little Sister' and 'His Latest Flame.'

Beyond the hit songs, movies were absorbing more and more of his energy. Released in December 1960 was the Twentieth Century Fox motion picture **Flaming Star**. In this classic film about tests of loyalty and racial prejudice, Elvis portrays Pacer Burton—a young man who is half Indian, half white. His co-stars included Barbara Eden, Dolores Del Rio and John McIntire. Elvis had a minor hit with the title song.

He returned home for Christmas—where Priscilla joined him, his father and his father's second wife, Davada 'Dee' Presley. Priscilla received a six-week-old 'hound dog' puppy of her own. She returned to her parents then, knowing that her platonic relationship with Elvis would one day culminate in marriage.

Elvis was to make just a few more personal appearances before taking a hiatus from touring that would last until 1968. The first two of these 'farewell tours' (but the fans didn't know it yet) took place in February 1961 at the Ellis Auditorium in Memphis. He was dressed in a white dinner jacket, tie and dark trousers, and the performances were surprisingly smooth and coolly sophisticated. A change was at hand, but no one could tell what it might be.

For the third, and last, of these performances, Elvis flew to Pearl Harbor, Hawaii, where the sold-out audience at Bloch Arena heard him sing 'Heartbreak Hotel,' 'Hound Dog,' 'Don't Be Cruel,' 'Treat Me Nice,' 'All Shook Up,' 'It's Now or Never,' 'That's All Right, Mama,' 'Are You Lonesome Tonight?' and many others of their favorite Elvis renditions. He wore dark trousers, an open-neck shirt and a golden jacket.

Elvis was now to devote himself entirely to his motion picture career.

Facing page and above: A face that none of his fans would see in live performance for most of the 1960s.

Above: Tuesday Weld, as 'Noreen,' in a scene with Elvis, as Glenn Tyler, from **Wild in the Country**, a Twentieth Century Fox release of June 1961. Elvis plays a confused, angry young man who is constantly in trouble with the law until psychotherapist Irene Sperry (Hope Lange) takes charge of him and helps him to straighten out.

Elvis, as Glenn Tyler, turns out to have some writing talent—this is yet one more challenge that he succeeds in meeting, but not before childhood sweetheart Betty Lee (played by Millie Perkins) has the struggle of her life trying to win Glenn over from his bad influences, which include the characters played by Ms Weld and another popular star, Gary Lockwood.

Above: An RCA Victor jacket cover for a '45' that featured the hit song 'Surrender,' backed with one of the tunes from **Wild in the Country**, 'Lonely Man'—which he sang in describing his predicament to Hope Lange. Other Elvis songs from **Wild in the Country** are 'I Slipped, I Stumbled, I Fell,' 'In My Way' and, of course, 'Wild In the Country.'

A little known fact is that, on 8 March 1961, the Tennessee legislature in Nashville made Elvis Presley an honorary Tennessee Colonel. While in Nashville for that ceremony, Elvis recorded the tunes that were to be included in **Wild in the Country** and his second motion picture of 1961, **Blue Hawaii**.

Above: Elvis as Chad Gates, and one of his many leading ladies in **Blue Hawaii**. Nancy Walters played Abigail Prentace, and Joan Blackman played Maile Duval, two of Elvis' romantic leads in the film.

The character Chad Gates is the restless son of a pineapple tycoon. Chad wants to make his own way in life—and after various difficulties succeeds in doing so. A Paramount release of November 1961, **Blue Hawaii** grossed $4.7 million, and was Elvis' most profitable film of that time.

The Tony Award-winning Angela Lansbury, as Sara Lee Gates, and Roland Winters, as Fred Gates, provided deft comic touches to this extremely light-hearted motion picture.

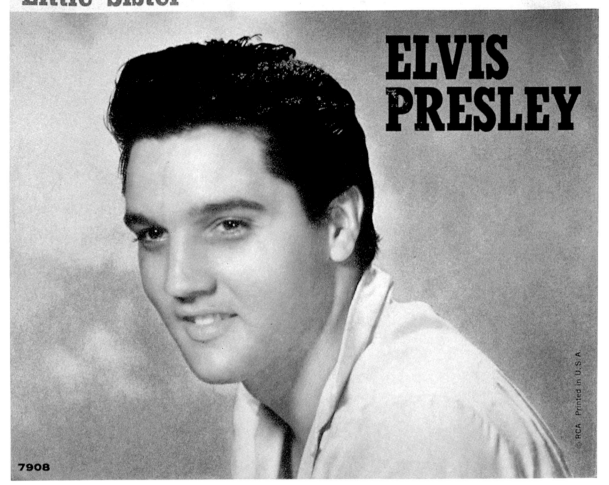

The soundtrack of **Blue Hawaii** includes the following tunes, which by their titles, fairly well outline the lightness of the movie: 'Blue Hawaii,' 'Almost Always True,' 'Shave 'n a Haircut — Two Bits,' 'Can't Help Falling in Love,' 'Rock-a-Hula Baby,' 'Ku-ou-i-po,' 'Beach Boy Blues,' 'Island of Love' and 'Hawaiian Wedding Song.'

Above: A record jacket for the RCA Victor 45 rpm release of the popular 'His Latest Flame,' backed with 'Little Sister' — both of which were available in record stores during the first run of **Blue Hawaii**, and both of which stood in contrast to the smooth, melodic ballads that were featured in the movie, and which would increasingly be the rule of the 'Elvis movie sound.'

After **Blue Hawaii**, Elvis' movie career skyrocketed, and the following years saw 'The King of Rock and Roll' getting deeper into this increasingly familiar milieu, in roles such as Toby Kwimper in **Follow That Dream** (United Artists, March 1962); Walter Gulick in **Kid Galahad** (United Artists, July 1962); Ross Carpenter in **Girls! Girls! Girls!** (featuring the hit song, 'Return to Sender'—Paramount, November 1962); Mike Edwards in **It Happened at the World's Fair** (Metro-Goldwyn-Mayer, November 1962) and as Mike Windgren in **Fun in Acapulco**. Then came a motion picture in which Elvis had not one, but *two*, roles.

Above: Two Elvises in one movie! Elvis is seen here in both of the roles he portrayed in the March 1964 Metro-Goldwyn-Mayer release, **Kissin' Cousins**. As Josh Morgan, he played a young Army officer whose job it is to roust a group of hillbillies from a proposed military site. Much to his surprise, he discovers a long-lost cousin, Jodie Tatum—whom he also portrays.

The romantic leads opposite Josh and Jodie are, respectively, Yvonne Craig, as 'hillbilly gal' Azalea Tatum; and Cynthia Pepper, as Midge, a WAC—who are seen with their partners in this photo. The film featured such Elvis renditions as 'Catchin' on Fast' and 'Smokey Mountain Boy.'

Above: Ann-Margret and Elvis in their roles as Lucky and Rusty, respectively, in the April 1964 release of **Viva Las Vegas**. Elvis, as Lucky, is an aspiring race car driver, and Ann-Margret's Rusty is a swimming instructor. Songs include a duet, 'The Lady Loves Me,' featuring the two stars.

Priscilla was by then living at Graceland, having graduated from high school the year before. The tensions caused by their living that closely—theirs was still a platonic relationship—were exacerbated by the many rumors drifting back from Hollywood, concerning Elvis and his off-stage activities with his co-star. It caused a rift between Priscilla and Elvis that was not easily healed.

It didn't ease Priscilla's mind at all that Ann-Margret was known in show business as 'the female Elvis Presley.'

Then came roles as Charlie Rogers, in **Roustabout** (Paramount, November 1964); Rusty Wells, in **Girl Happy** (Metro-Goldwyn-Mayer, January 1965); Lonnie Beale, in **Tickle Me**; and as Johnny Tyronne in **Harum Scarum**.

Immediately after **Harum Scarum** came **Frankie and Johnny**, a United Artists release of July 1966.

Above: Elvis, as Johnny, and Nancy Novack, as Nelly Bly, keep their eyes on the roulette wheel as Harry Morgan, as the croupier Cully, waits to call the winner.

Included in **Frankie and Johnny** are Elvis' renditions of 'The Ballad of Frankie and Johnny,' 'When the Saints Go Marchin' In,' 'Broadway' and 'Beginner's Luck.' It was the twentieth of a total of 33 films he would make.

Facing page: Elvis in character, in a publicity still from **Harum Scarum**. This film was released by Metro-Goldwyn-Mayer in December 1965. Elvis' premier backup group, The Jordanaires, were on hand to add texture to such musical numbers as 'Go East, Young Man.'

Above: This is the Elvis his fans saw with decreasing regularity in the 1960s: relaxed and accessible. Since he began concentrating exclusively on movie making in the early 1960s, Elvis had become a recluse—living at Graceland with his fiancee, Priscilla, and making regular sojourns to Hollywood for motion picture production.

Seen with Elvis in this photograph is Steve Forrest, who played the part of Clint Burton in one of Elvis' finest films, **Flaming Star** (see text, page 47).

Even with a tendency to hole up in Graceland, the King found time for
one of his favorite pursuits—taking jaunts by car. He preferred to drive
himself, and in the mid-to-late 1960s, often drove for hours after dark in
a custom-built Cadillac with Priscilla.

It was an echoing of a habit he'd developed while still the up-and-
coming rock and roller. He often worked himself up so much on stage
that he would drive around restlessly—well into the wee morning
hours—in order to calm down.

Above: A timeless photograph—'The King' behind the wheel of a
chariot fit for a king: a classic 1955 Ford Thunderbird.

During the course of making his many motion pictures, Elvis became a remarkably adept balladeer (given his earlier, more flamboyant singing style), with finely crafted renditions of 'Can't Help Falling in Love,' 'Forget Me Never,' 'I Need Somebody to Lean On,' 'Please Don't Stop Loving Me,' 'I'll Remember You' and 'Love Letters in the Sand.'

Above: No matter what stage of his career he was in, however, Elvis always had his fans. Here a bevy of adoring teenagers happily pose with him for a publicity still.

Facing page: Elvis in an earlier time, surrounded by the adulation of crewcut boys, and girls in curlers.

Above and below: Elvis the international ambassador of goodwill. Elvis never left the United States to perform, yet he has a huge world-wide following to this day. Here, we see him at an international soiree, mingling with guests of various nationalities.

Facing page: Elvis was an avid student of religious philosophy, never really settling on one—yet he would return in several albums to his First Assembly of God Church roots (see text, page 89).

A study in contrasts.

Above: Elvis in his free-wheeling, pre-Army days, and...

Facing page: Elvis at the airport with the love of his life, Priscilla. He met her while he was in the Army (see text, page 38), and somehow, his life hadn't been quite the same afterward.

As can be seen, Priscilla adopted one of the two fashion extremes that were popular in the latter 1960s. The other extreme was strictly no makeup; no permanent wave for the hair; and attire that consisted of blouse and blue jeans or a simple 'granny dress.' According to her autobiographical book, *Elvis and Me*, he liked her this way. Especially, he requested she dye her hair black to 'show off' her blue eyes more.

Priscilla and Elvis get married. The decision was made just before Christmas of 1966, and Elvis 'pledged his troth' by giving Priscilla a 3.5-carat diamond engagement ring. In February 1967, Elvis bought a 160-acre ranch, which he named the 'Circle G' (for Graceland) near Horn Lake, Mississippi—at which he and his bride-to-be hoped to spend many happy retreats together. On 1 May 1967, after the happy couple spent a brief sojourn in Palm Springs, California, they flew east to Las Vegas, Nevada, obtained a marriage license, and were married at 9:41 am by Justice of the Nevada Supreme Court David Zenoff.

A formal ceremony and reception followed, at Las Vegas' Aladdin Hotel. Both of these events were finely orchestrated by Colonel Parker.

Above: Elvis and Priscilla, just after exchanging marital vows.

Facing page: The newlyweds prepare to cut their cake at the reception.

Above: The rice rains down as Elvis and Priscilla Presley prepare to embark on their honeymoon. Frank Sinatra lent them his private jet to fly back to Palm Springs and their rented house there. A few days later, they went for a stay at the Circle G Ranch.

Originally, plans were made to elude the press and the inevitable crush of well-meaning fans. This they did do — but immediately after the wedding and reception, a press conference was held, and then again, there were reporters to contend with at their Palm Springs house.

Elvis handled it all with grace and charm, despite the momentous occasion that had at last dawned for 'Mr and Mrs Elvis Presley.' Seven years and eight months after their August 1959, meeting at the Eagles Club in West Germany, a mutual dream had been fulfilled.

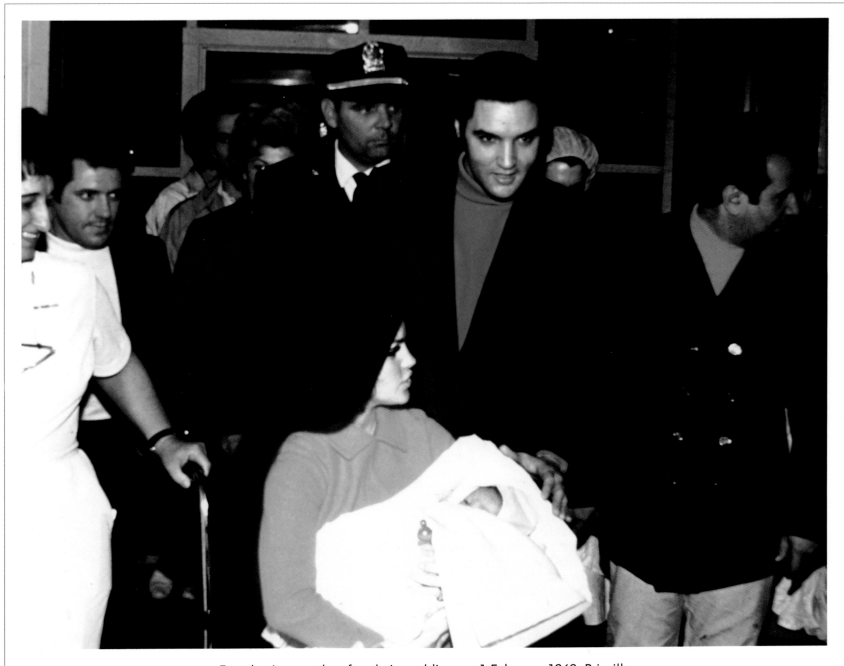

Exactly nine months after their wedding, on 1 February 1968, Priscilla gave birth to Lisa Marie Presley at Baptist Memorial Hospital in Memphis. Elvis immediately assumed the role of the doting father, and hovered around mother and child protectively. Lisa Marie was to be their only child.

Above: Lisa Marie and her mom and dad emerge from Baptist Memorial Hospital. Such bliss, however, was not long to last: by 1970, both parents were having difficulties with their spouse.

In addition to his marriage and parenthood, the mid-to-late 1960s were very active cinematically for Elvis. After the completion of **Paradise, Hawaiian Style** (Paramount, June 1966), he had starring roles in **Spinout** (Metro-Goldwyn-Mayer, December 1966); **Easy Come, Easy Go** (Paramount, June 1967); **Double Trouble** (Metro-Goldwyn Mayer, May 1967); **Clambake** (United Artists, December 1967); **Stay Away, Joe** (with Burgess Meredith and Joan Blondell) (Metro-Goldwyn-Mayer, March 1968); **Speedway** (with Nancy Sinatra) (Metro-Goldwyn-Mayer, June 1968); **Live a Little, Love a Little** (Metro-Goldwyn-Mayer, October 1968); **Charro!** (National General Productions, Incorporated, September 1969); and **The Trouble With Girls** (with Sheree North, Vincent Price and John Carradine) (Metro-Goldwyn-Mayer, December 1969).

His millions of fans, however, wanted to see Elvis live — and singing. He made his comeback on the concert stage via television. The show was taped between 27 and 29 June 1968, and was aired on 3 December of that same year. It was a smash hit, and was a precursor of Elvis' blossoming forth as a musician once again. The special featured the brand-new million seller 'If I Can Dream,' and a plethora of such Elvis classics as 'Heartbreak Hotel,' 'Don't be Cruel,' 'Jailhouse Rock' and 'Are You Lonesome Tonight?'

Above: In an earlier, simpler time. Elvis as Clint and Debra Paget as Cathy in a publicity still for **Love Me Tender** (Twentieth Century Fox, November 1956). The theme song Elvis sang in that film was aptly titled 'Love Me Tender,' and was a big hit. It had been adapted from an American folk ballad entitled 'Ora Lee.' *At right:* Elvis in a meditative mood.

In January and February of 1969, Elvis was a veritable whirlwind of creativity, spinning out more hits than he had since his earlier musical heyday of the late 1950s. In a series of RCA recording sessions in Memphis, he laid down tracks for 'In the Ghetto,' 'Suspicious Minds' and 'Kentucky Rain,' among many other renditions evidencing vitality and inventiveness that meant unequivocably that 'The King of Rock and Roll' was back.

Above: Elvis and his fans: an image that has become *Americana*.

Above: Elvis and an enthusiastic fan, backstage. The King wanted to tour, and Colonel Parker set up a contract for him to perform at Las Vegas' International Hotel for two shows per night for 28 days. His opening night was the first strictly live performance he had given in nine years: it was a triumph, featuring 'All Shook Up,' 'Blue Suede Shoes,' 'Tiger Man,' 'In the Ghetto' and other renditions that were a veritable cross-section of his musical career. Even Colonel Parker had tears in his eyes.

Elvis was, however, to star in three more motion pictures — **Change of Habit** (with Mary Tyler Moore)(NBC-Universal, January 1970); **Elvis: That's the Way It Is** (Metro-Goldwyn-Mayer, December 1970); and **Elvis on Tour** (Metro-Goldwyn-Mayer, October 1972). These latter two were documentaries of Elvis on concert tour, and in and of themselves are still highly regarded. **Elvis on Tour** won the Golden Globe Award for Best Documentary of 1972.

Above: At home, Elvis was full of jokes, just as he was on the stage—witness his legendary slow, romantic buildup to one of the most riotous rock songs of all time: '...and then I told her... "You ain't nothin' but a hound dog!"'

His effect on audiences was as legendary as his sense of humor. On 30 July 1954, Elvis had his first professional public appearance as an adult (see text, page 6) at Overton Park Bandshell in Memphis.

He launched into a steaming rendition of 'That's All Right, Mama'—and to his shock, teenagers at the back of the theater started screaming. Said Elvis: 'I was scared, I didn't understand it.... I slept badly that night... nightmares full of screaming people... but they weren't frightening because I knew that those screams meant the end of money worries for Mom and Dad.'

Above: Elvis prepares for a nighttime drive, with Graceland in the background. Said Elvis of his first Cadillac, bought for $5000 in 1955: 'Man, this is livin'.'

His motto for running the affairs of Graceland was 'Taking care of business—in a flash!' This explains the acronym, 'TCB' emblazoned at various locations throughout Graceland.

His first recording session at Sun records, back in 1953, went unnoticed. With the second session, Elvis, intent on singing slow ballads, tried a fast rhythm and blues number during a break to make his friends laugh. Sun Records' owner, Sam Phillips, said: 'Boy, that's great! That's how you gotta sing!' And so, the style of Elvis Presley, the *definitive* rock and roll star, was born.

Above: Elvis and his father, Vernon Presley.

Facing page: Elvis in a publicity still.

Elvis never lost the habit of consulting his father for advice. Vernon was, in fact, Elvis' chief financial officer—a position that his Great Depression-born penuriousness recommended him to. Yet, in the final analysis, he could never refuse Elvis.

The Circle G Ranch (see text, page 66) was a case in point. At $500,000, Vernon thought it was not a good deal—yet Elvis pressed the idea, saying 'I'm having fun, Daddy, for the first time in ages.' Vernon capitulated.

Father and son maintained a virtually unguarded, life-long intimacy.

Above: A scene from **Double Trouble**, the 1967 Metro-Goldwyn-Mayer release in which Elvis portrayed disco singer Guy Lambert, an otherwise happy-go-lucky fellow who is pursued through Belgium by a literal mob of people—some of whom love him and some of whom want to kill him. This was oddly analogous to Elvis' own life.

There were death threats, and fans literally hurling themselves at him. At one show, a woman crashed into the drums—a human guided missile that Elvis sidestepped with the grace of a survivor.

In addition, his marriage to the girl of his dreams ended in divorce on 9 October 1973. Priscilla and Elvis were said to be on personally friendly terms, but even so, Elvis was admitted to Baptist Memorial hospital just a few days later for hypertension.

Double Trouble, and all films like it, were far in Elvis' past by the time his revived concert career was in full swing. In 1972, for instance, he toured 15 cities in April, eight cities in June and seven cities in September and set an all-time attendance record at New York City's Madison Square Garden of 80,000 ticket-holders for a three-concert run.

Facing page: Elvis Presley, evincing that mixture of strength and utter vulnerability that his fans found irresistable.

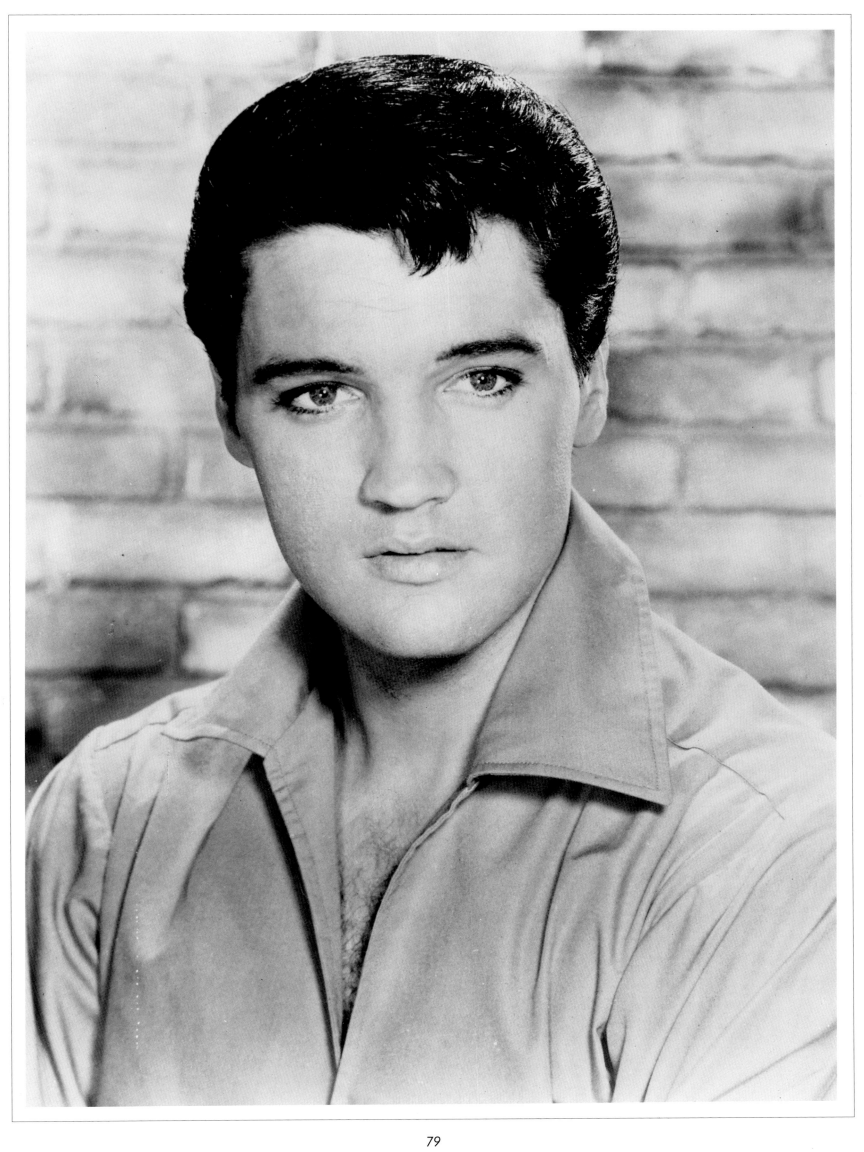

Above: Elvis loosens up on a set of drums, during a break in the filming of **Flaming Star** (see text, page 47)—somewhere on the Twentieth Century Fox studio lot in 1960.

The eponymous hit song from **Flaming Star** aptly described Elvis' meteoric rise to fame, and the intensity with which he conducted his concert tours. While the moviemaking period was busy enough (Elvis made an average of three motion pictures per year from 1964—68), his concert touring had become more than any other human being would normally attempt: between 17 March 1975 and 1 January 1976, for instance, Elvis' tour included 74 cities.

Facing page: The face that launched a thousand screams!

Speedway, on the other hand, had no relation to *anyone's* reality at all. A piece of fluff blown into production by some director's snore, this was typical of the kind of motion picture that made so many people yawn when overhearing mention of an 'Elvis movie.' While it *is* true that Elvis starred in a number of entertaining films (**King Creole**, **Jailhouse Rock** and **Flaming Star**, to name a few), only his immense and lasting popularity made throwaways like **Speedway** moneymakers.

As we know, that situation didn't last. When his last movie contract ran out, Elvis very happily went back to putting on his *own kind* of show. His song selection eventually included 'Proud Mary,' 'Polk Salad Annie' and slower numbers such as 'Bridge Over Troubled Water,' 'Let Me Be There' and the stupendous 'American Trilogy' — a medley of 'Dixie,' 'The Battle Hymn of the Republic' and 'All My Trials.'

Above: A scene from **Speedway** (also, see text, page 70).

Facing page: A late-1950s — early 1960s publicity photo featuring Elvis and a moderate portion of his daily fan mail.

Above: Elvis as Greg, and Michelle Carey as Bernice, in **Live a Little, Love a Little** (see also text, page 70). Legendary crooner Rudy Vallee also starred in this film about the romantic entanglements of bachelor photographer Greg.

In this photo, Michelle Carey seems to be perpetrating some sort of psychic healing on Elvis' ankle, while he seems to be mentally elsewhere. It was late 1968, and Elvis' thoughts were turning wholeheartedly toward live concerts—and away from the entanglements of motion picture studio productions.

Las Vegas was to become his concert 'home' (Elvis appeared there in July 1969; January 1970; August 1970; January 1971; July—September 1971; January 1972; February 1973 (cancelled due to illness); and had several extended appearances in 1974, 1975 and 1976. Beyond this, he had an extensive touring schedule (see text, page 81).

Facing page: A golden portrait.

That his career as a singer was far more important to him than his career as an actor is evident in the fact that Elvis planned and rehearsed for two months in preparation for his television comeback special (see also text, page 70). It was said that he worked harder during these rehearsals than he did for *any* of his movies. It was the highest-rated special of the year, garnering an overwhelming share of the television audience for the night of its showing on 3 December 1969.

The show was directed by Steve Binder, a young director whose sympathetic approach helped ease Elvis' tension. Elvis, of course, orchestrated the musical part of the show, while Binder and others worked out the logistics, camera angles and so on.

Facing page: Elvis in the midst of a soulful rendition, during the 1969 NBC special that marked his return to the concert stage. Elvis' black leather suit was created by costume designer Bill Belew, and, sleek as it looks, Elvis was still moved to confide in Priscilla: 'I feel a little silly in that outfit. You think it's okay?'

For that 50-minute show, he performed in the midst of a small studio audience. The album that he recorded immediately afterward in Memphis, *From Elvis in Memphis* (RCA Victor, 1969) was a winner, and a string of hits followed (see text, page 70). Never again would Elvis be solely an image on the screen at the local movie theater.

Above: Elvis in performance in 1969—70. He was back to dressing flashy — a hallmark of his pre-Hollywood career, when he became 'The King of Rock and Roll.' The sideburns, also a hallmark of those days, made a comeback, too.

Here, he has obviously gained an aggressiveness that is almost wholly lacking in his later motion pictures. The Elvis we see here is obviously — and totally — involved with his performance.

His live performances were all sold out, and his television appearances reached even larger audiences. On 14 January 1973, for instance, his **Aloha From Hawaii** show was simulcast from Honolulu to 40 countries worldwide, reaching an estimated 500 *million* viewers.

With hits like 'Big Boss Man' and 'Burnin' Love,' Elvis' sound filled the airwaves again. His 'sound' was based on the same dictum he'd always followed: the band had to be as prominent as the singer: 'It adds mystery,' he said, 'they can't tell what I'm singin' and they listen closer.'

Rock singers down through the years have acknowledged his influence: 'Without Elvis,' said Buddy Holly, 'none of us could have made it.' 'That Elvis, man....He wrote the book,' says Bruce Springsteen.

Elvis won the first of his four Grammy Awards in 1967 for the album *How Great Thou Art*, which featured gospel songs that he had probably first heard in his youth, when the Presleys were in the congregation of the First Assembly of God Church. *How Great Thou Art* went on to win an unusual *second* Grammy in 1974.

A very special Grammy for Elvis was The Bing Crosby Award in 1971, 'for creative contributions of outstanding artistic or scientific significance.' Another gospel album, *He Touched Me* (with The Imperials doing Elvis' backup vocals, and using their arrangements), won yet another Grammy in 1972.

Sincerely Yours
Elvis

Elvis' stage moves were born out of the crowd's reaction. When he made a move on stage, if it got a positive reaction, it stayed in his act. It often worked too well. Marty Robbins recalls being in Jacksonville, Florida during one Elvis performance in the 1950s: 'They chased him into the dressing room and he was up on top of the showers trying to get away from people, girls and guys alike. They were trying to grab a shoe, anything….'

Above: Elvis in performance.

Facing page: An autographed portrait of Elvis in the midst of a ballad.

Above: Elvis in costume as reformed outlaw Jess Wade in **Charro!** (see text, page 70). This film might well have have been waggishly dubbed 'Double Stubble,' as it is the only motion picture in which Elvis sported a beard. The pistol fits one of Elvis' personal interests perfectly, however — he was an avid fan of law enforcement and crime detection — in fact, he was made an official federal narcotics officer on 21 December 1970 by US President Richard Milhous Nixon.

While such films were considered a waste by some reviewers, others felt that Elvis had gained maturity through his Hollywood experience. In 1971, Elvis was named the world's top male singer by Great Britain's highly respected musical weekly, the *New Musical Express*. But then again, this was no surprise — it was the twelfth time in 13 years that Elvis had won the honor.

Indeed, Britain's own 'top male singers' adulated Elvis. Said Mick Jagger: 'Elvis was an original in an arena of imitators.'

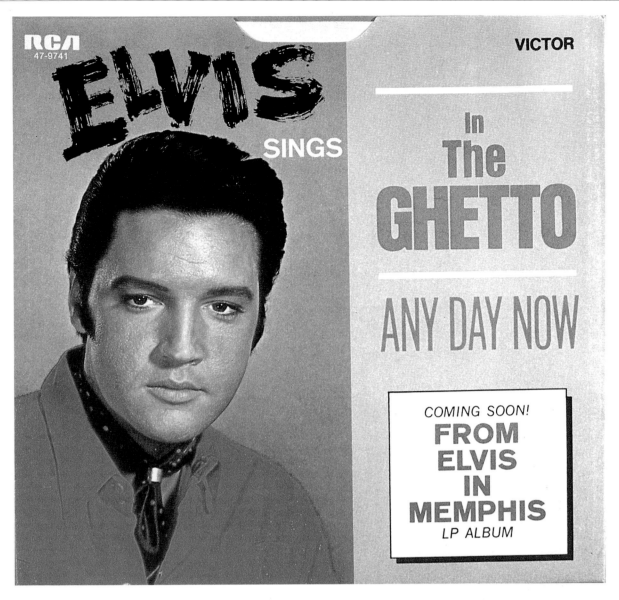

Above: The dust jacket for a 45 rpm release of Elvis' legendary hit, 'In the Ghetto,' backed with 'Any Day Now.' Note the advance notice for his smash-hit comeback album, *From Elvis in Memphis* (see text, page 86). The album wiped away the years Elvis had spent in Hollywood, away from the music business. It was as sustained and striking as anything he had ever done.

From Elvis in Memphis contained, in addition to the two hits just mentioned, 'Only the Strong Survive,' 'Gentle on My Mind,' 'Power of My Love,' 'After Loving You,' 'One Night,' 'True Love Travels on a Gravel Road,' 'It Keeps Right On A-Hurtin',' 'Movin' On,' 'Long Black Limousine,' 'I'll Hold You in My Heart.'

It was no secret, of course, that rock superstars (such as Mick Jagger, Rod Stewart, Janis Joplin and many, many others) of the late 1960s and early 1970s were avid collectors—and *students*—of Elvis' early material (see text, pages 10, 14, 22, 45 – 48)—much of which can be found on two RCA albums entitled *A Date With Elvis* and *For LP Fans Only*.

With *From Elvis in Memphis*, they had yet another Himalayan mountain to inspect in their ever-attentive search for 'perfection in pop.' Let us not forget, however, that Elvis' versatility was such that he became the first musician in history to top three major charts—Pop; Rhythm & Blues; and Country & Western.

Above: In an image from **Elvis: That's the Way It Is**, Elvis rehearses with his band. On 22 September 1970, Elvis recorded four songs: 'Snowbird,' 'Whole Lotta Shakin' Goin' On,' 'Rags to Riches' and 'Where Did They Go, Lord?' The former two were kept on hold for a later album, and the latter two were released as a single in March 1971. The session was cut short, however, as Elvis' increasingly light-sensitive eyes began to hurt—he increasingly suffered from a mild case of glaucoma, which necessitated his wearing dark eyeglasses or tinted contact lenses for much of the time.

Facing page: Elvis, on tour, as represented in one of the two documentaries that featured 'his act on the road.' This is another image from **Elvis: That's the Way It Is** (Metro-Goldwyn-Mayer, released December 1970).

Above: The marquee of the Las Vegas Hilton, sometime in the early 1970s. The Hilton was Elvis' concert venue for more than 30 weeks between January 1971 and December 1976. Following in the footsteps of Elvis and other popular greats, Charlie Rich—whose name is featured on the left wing of this enormous marquee—began his recording career in the late 1950s.

However—sartorially, Elvis seemed to be following in the footsteps of the dandified Liberace, whose name appears on the right wing of the marquee. As the 1970s progressed, Elvis' costumes became increasingly elaborate and ostentatious.

When he was beginning his comeback in the late 1960s, however, the Elvis 'look' was streamlined and clean, allowing for maximum movement and immediate visual impact.

Above, he wears the white suit that he sometimes alternated with his black leather togs. The object wasn't *what* Elvis was *wearing* after all, but what he was *doing* while he was wearing it. For some fans, that didn't even matter—it was sufficient that Elvis exist, and proximity made it all the better.

RCA kept an ongoing catalogue of Elvis' recorded products, called *The Complete Catalogue of Elvis Records and Tapes*. It contained, as of 1970, more than 30 pages of albums, tapes, cartridges and cassettes—and most of this was in stock at the average community music store. In August 1970, RCA issued a four-record album of Elvis' 50 most popular songs, entitled *Elvis' Worldwide 50 Gold Award Hits, Volume I* (which would be in the best-selling charts for months, from 1970—1971). In October, RCA released a double album entitled *From Memphis to Vegas/From Vegas to Memphis*, which was actually a repackaging of two albums from the year before—*Elvis in Person at the International Hotel* and *Elvis Back in Memphis*.

On 19 December 1970, Elvis Presley had a spat with his family, and left Graceland on his own — something he hadn't done in a long time, being a man with an extensive entourage.

After a day of wandering around, he contacted his publicist Jerry Schilling, and on 21 December 1970, the two took a jet to Washington, DC. On the jet, Elvis gave a soldier who was homeward bound for the holidays $500 in cash — all the money he had on him at the time — because the soldier was 'going home for Christmas. I want to make it a good one for him and his loved ones....The guy just got back from Vietnam.'

Then, revealing his true agenda, Elvis hastily scrawled a letter to President of the United States Richard Milhous Nixon, asking to be made a federal narcotics officer. In Washington, he presented the letter to the White House security officer, and almost immediately received an audience with the President, who granted his request with a flourish and a handshake (above).

Facing page: Elvis at a cashier's window in his early career. He was known for his generosity — at one point buying a house for his publicist Jerry Schilling, and on many instances giving away cars, jewelry and other expensive items to those he cared for, or felt to be in need.

These pages: Images of Elvis in some of his many concerts. Probably his most extravagant were the two concerts that formed the substance for his **Aloha from Hawaii** telecast (see also text on page 88), in January 1973. The concerts were held in the Hilton Hawaiian Dome in Honolulu. Dress rehearsal the night before the first of the two concerts was crammed with an estimated 10,000 people.

The show was in part a fund-raiser for the Kui Lee Cancer Fund, and Colonel Parker pressured celebrities such as Jack Lord, star of the television series **Hawaii Five-O**, to contribute $1000 for their concert seats, while many children got in for a penny. The two shows raised $85,000 for the charity.

The production of the show cost $2.5 million, which made the telecast the most expensive entertainment special produced to that date. The show was hugely popular—if viewer polls in Japan were any measure: there, **Aloha From Hawaii** captured 98 percent of the television audience. In addition, Elvis was paid a million dollars for his two hours in concert, easily setting a new precedent for concert earnings.

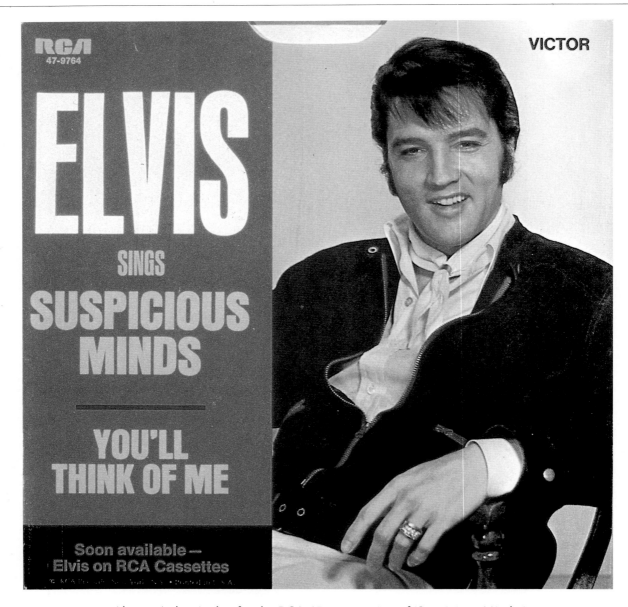

Above: A dust jacket for the RCA 45 rpm version of 'Suspicious Minds,' backed with 'You'll Think of Me.' RCA produced countless singles and *at least* three Elvis albums per year in the 1970s.

In sessions at RCA's Memphis studios in March and May of 1971, he laid tracks for—among other numbers—'Early Morning Rain,' Bob Dylan's classic 'Don't Think Twice, It's All Right' and 'Merry Christmas, Baby.' All in all, more than 35 songs were recorded.

That same year, seven Elvis albums were released. In addition to those mentioned on page 97, there were *Elvis: The Other Sides, Worldwide 50 Gold Award Hits, Volume II; Elvis Country* (featuring Elvis renditions of hits made famous by country music artists Billy Walker, Patsy Cline, Eddy Arnold and others); *The Wonderful World of Christmas; You'll Never Walk Alone;* and *C'mon Everybody.*

Five more albums were released in 1972, including *Elvis Sings Hits From His Movies, Volume I; Burnin' Love and Hits From His Movies, Volume II*—both of which were big money makers, and the latter of which stayed on the album charts for six months. Also, Elvis won a Grammy that year for his gospel music (see text, page 89).

So it went on through the 1970s, and the 1980s—one can still purchase almost any item from the Presley *oeuvre* from the corner record store in 'Anytown, USA.' As they say in the business, Elvis Presley hits have extremely long 'shelf lives.'

Facing page: 'The King' in mid-song.

Above: Elvis, cooling down after giving fans his usual 110 percent at a concert.

Facing page: Elvis, during his 20-minute press conference just prior to the historic Madison Square Garden concerts in June 1972 (see also text, page 78). The gross from these concerts was $750,000.

Among the featured songs were 'Polk Salad Annie' and 'That's All Right, Mama': Elvis did a little bit of everything in his repertoire. Critic Robert Palmer, writing his appreciation of the 'live' album that resulted from these Madison Square Garden shows, said: 'Everybody gets enough of what they want to get....'

It has been said that Elvis sought to please everybody, and with his extraordinary versatility, he succeeded. As critic Robert Christgau wrote: 'He enticed me into communion with people whose values were very unlike my own.'

Facing page: Priscilla went from her marriage with Elvis to a career of her own, including the role of Jenna Wade on the television series **Dallas**. She authored (with Sandra Harmon) a book on her life with Elvis, entitled *Elvis and Me,* which was first published in 1985, and was immediately at the top of the best-seller lists.

Priscilla also had a full-time occupation in raising her and Elvis' daughter, Lisa Marie—who is shown *above* with her husband Danny Keough at an art gallery in Los Angeles in 1987.

Elvis, wherever he truly is, may well be glad that he's a *grandfather*— for, with the arrival in this world of seven-pound, two-ounce Danielle Riley Keough on 29 May 1989, both he and Priscilla have ample reason to be proud of their daughter, and *her* daughter.

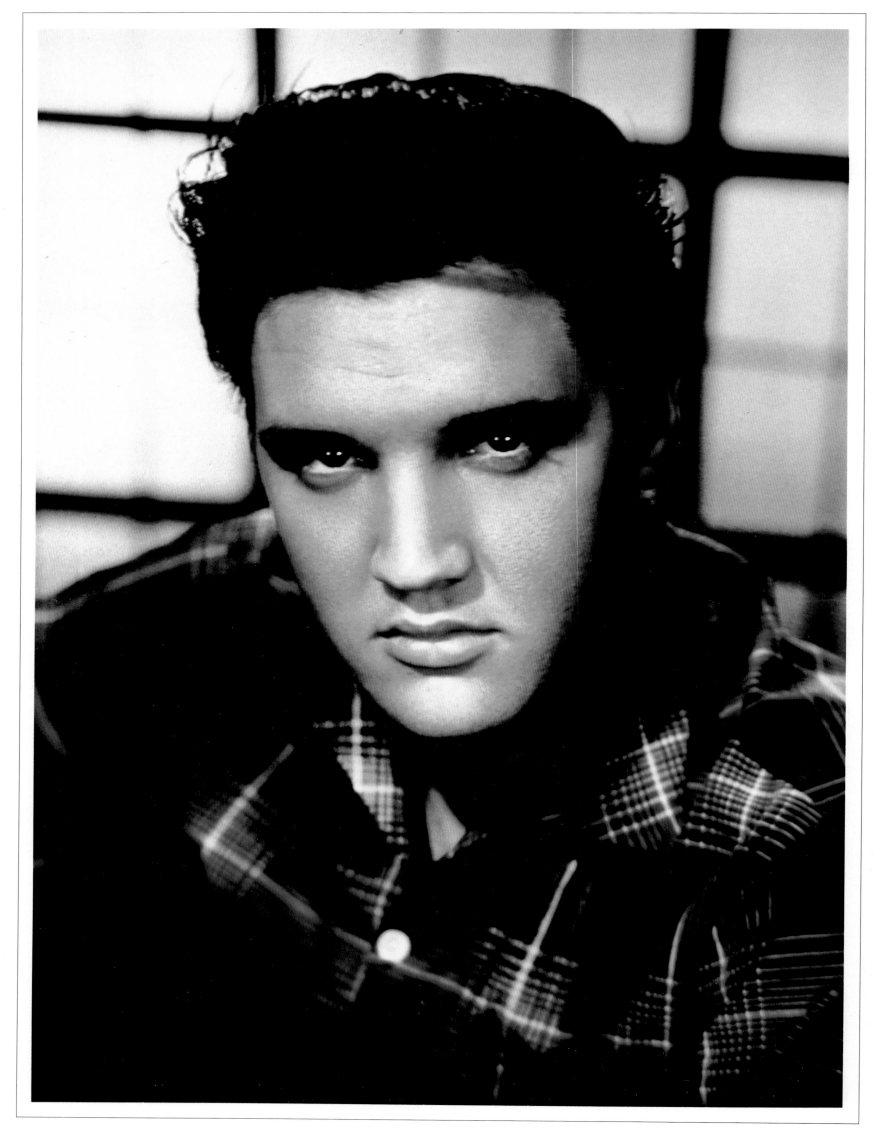

His records, tapes, movies, videotapes—and endless other spinoffs from his creative efforts are hot market items to this very day. What can be said about the seminal figure of rock-and-roll music as it is known and enjoyed by billions of fans world wide?

The man who made the words 'hound dog' resonate so that fans shrieked and fainted—not so much for the song, as for the fact that Elvis was talented enough to make it appear that he *believed* the song as he sang it, and entranced his audiences into sharing that conviction. When he was on stage, Elvis was committed to giving it all he had.

Above: A youthful fan poses near a plaque that is *believed to be* a synopsis of the entire story of Elvis Presley. One feels there is a chapter or two that is yet to be written.

Facing page: Elvis in the late 1950s, with that 'do or die' stare that has so often been copied by pretenders to his title of 'The King of Rock and Roll.'

Index

Facing page: Elvis as he is envisioned by his many fans. Among the spate of his albums released in the mid-1970s are *Good Times* and *Pure Gold*—yet perhaps it is a three-album series that most aptly describes him in his entirety: *Elvis—A Legendary Performer.*

Overleaf: Elvis' star still shines bright on Hollywood Boulevard.